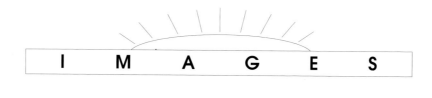

Blue

Karen Bryant-Mole

Silver Press
Parsippany, New Jersey

First published in Great Britain by Heinemann Library, an imprint of
Heinemann Publishers (Oxford) Ltd., Halley Court, Jordan Hill, Oxford OX2 8EJ, U.K.

© BryantMole Books 1996
Designed by Jean Wheeler
Commissioned photography by Zul Mukhida
Printed in Hong Kong
00 99 98 97 96
10 9 8 7 6 5 4 3 2 1

Published in the United States in 1997 by Silver Press
A Division of Simon & Schuster
299 Jefferson Road
Parsippany, NJ 07054

Library of Congress Cataloging-in-Publication Data

Bryant-Mole, Karen.
   Blue/by Karen Bryant-Mole.
     p. cm. — (Images)
  Includes index.
   Summary: Photographs of such things as a plate, toy boat, and buttons introduce the
color blue.
  ISBN 0-382-39590-5 (LSB) — ISBN 0-382-39626-X (pbk)
   1. Blue — Juvenile literature. 2. Color — Juvenile literature. 3. Colors — Juvenile literature.
[1. Blue. 2. Color.] I. Title. II. Series: Bryant-Mole, Karen.
QC 495.5. B79 1996   95-51089
535.6 — dc20   CIP
                                              AC

Some of the more difficult words in this book are explained in the glossary.

Acknowledgments
The Publishers would like to thank the following for permission to reproduce photographs. Chapel Studios, 23 (right);
Zul Mukhida, Oxford Scientific Films, 8 (right); Richard Day, 9 (left); Lawrence Migdale Photo Researchers Inc,
9 (right); Tom Ulrich, 23 (left); David Shale, Tony Stone Images, 8 (left); Schafer & Hill, 16 (left); Martyn Goddard,
17 (left); Alan Levenson, 17 (right); Martyn Goddard, 22 (right); Rex A Butcher, Zefa, 16 (right), 22 (left).

Every effort had been made to contact copyright holders of any material reproduced in this book. Any omissions will be
rectified in subsequent printings if notice is given to the Publisher.

Contents

Clothes

Are you wearing anything blue today?

4

Bath time

a sponge

bubble
bath

Do you like bubbles
in your bath?

a washcloth

a boat

soap

Birds

Have you ever seen
a bluebird?

Toys

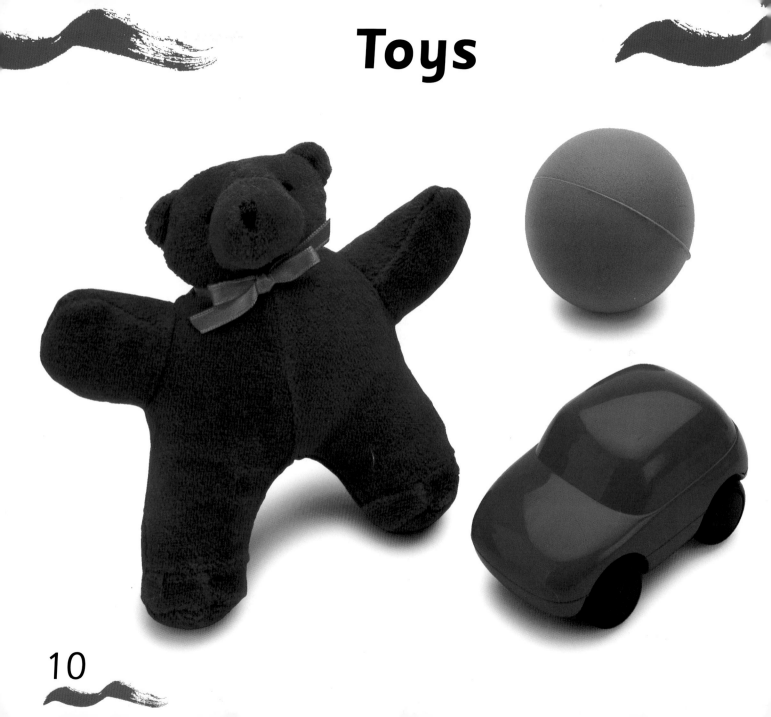

Here are some blue toys.

Do you have any blue toys?

Breakfast

a spoon

a cup

a bowl

a plate

a knife

13

Do you like
building sand castles?

This bucket
makes a castle
with towers.

On the move

a tractor

a jeep

a truck

a car

Babies

Babies often have their own special things.

18

You probably had some of these
when you were a baby!

Buttons

Buttons are used to fasten clothing.

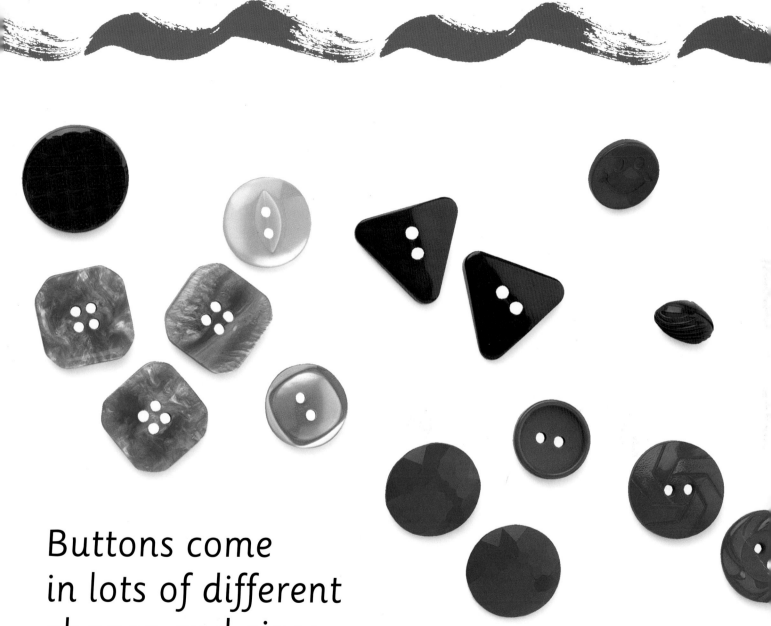

Buttons come
in lots of different
shapes and sizes.

Flowers

Here are some
blue flowers.

Glossary

jeep   a vehicle that can ride over fields and rough ground as well as on the road

washcloth   a special piece of cloth used to wash your body

Index